KINGDOM DISCIPLESHIP

PART 3

MULTIPLYING DISCIPLES

L. Douglas Dorman, Ph.D.

LEADER SPACE

ALIGNING HEARTS WITH GOD'S PERSPECTIVE

Kingdom Discipleship - Part 3: Multiplying Disciples

Published by LeaderSpace

Consultant and Cover Layout: Kelly Smith, Tallgrass Media
Cover Art: Lottie Dorman

Book Layout: Lori Michelle
www.TheAuthorsAlley.com

Paperback ISBN: 978-1-956589-05-4

TABLE OF CONTENTS

Encourage and Empower Nationals
Support One Another
Train pastors, leaders, and church planters
Take Risk
Evangelizing
Announcing the Kingdom
Multiply

Dedicated to Joan Dorman

Week 1 Day 1
Review of Section 1:
Being a Disciple

This week we will review Sections 1—3, on days 1, 2, and 3; plus, we will expand on discipleship by outlining CORE discipleship on Day 4, and we will explore the importance of Surrender on Day 5.

The Your Next Step Vision
- *Bring them in*
- *Build them up*
- *Send them out*
- *Publicly, and*
- *House to House*

Bring them in

The Father draws people to himself in John 6:44. He invites us to join him in seeking and saving the lost in Luke 19:10.

"And he said to them, *'Follow me, and I will make you fishers of men.'*" **Matthew 4:19 ESV**

Build them up

God desires for us to live fruitful lives, see John 15. Our calling goes beyond our own growth, God invites us to help others grow in the faith; we facilitate kingdom growth by building others up, see 1 Corinthians 3:9-10. God grows his kids in relational communities, see Ephesians 2:19-22.

1

Send them out

The Father sends the Son, the Father and Son send the Spirit, the triune God sends us. God invites us to go out and proclaim the good news of the kingdom in John 17:18.

Publicly

Why do we use the symbol of the shepherd's staff to represent our public function? The motif of the shepherd shows up repeatedly in the scripture. Moses and David, two Old Testament leaders, shepherd sheep before they shepherd people, see Psalm 78:72. David refers to the LORD as his shepherd in Psalm 23. In the New Testament, the angels announce Jesus' birth to shepherds first. Jesus calls himself the good shepherd in John 10:11. Moses, David, and Jesus serve in public arenas as servant leaders, shepherds of God's people. God invites us to shepherd others by providing protection, showing kindness, gentleness, and love as a shepherdess or shepherd does for her or his sheep, see Acts 20:20, 28.

House to House

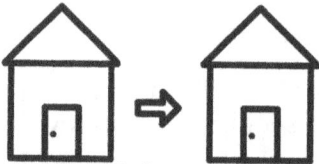

Jesus ministers in public spaces like open air gatherings, in the Temple, and in synagogues. He also frequents homes. Paul's ministry utilizes public spaces and private homes as well, see Acts 20:20. For the first 200 years of the church, homes serve as meeting locations.

The Greek word "Oikos" translates as household; oikos shows up throughout the pages of the New Testament. Using our homes as hospitality centers reflects the heart of God—a heart of welcome, a place of community. The home provides the best context for disciple making, see Romans 12:13. Understanding the centrality of the home helps us understand the biblical focus on hospitality, welcome, sharing meals together, the use of spiritual gifts, and the "one anothers" of scripture; these functions flow best—then and now—in homes.

PART 3: MULTIPLYING DISCIPLES

Key Passage

In Kingdom Discipleship—Part 1—Being A Disciple, we unpacked 1 John 2:12-14.

Read 1 John 2:12-14 again. Also, in Part 1, we introduced three key illustrations.

- Three Trees
- 10 Periods
- Stop, Look, Listen

JOURNAL TIME

What do you notice when you read 1 John 2:12-14?

Look back at Your Next Step's vision. Write out the vision using your own words.

Week 1 Day 2
Walking in Freedom

"So if the Son makes you free, you will be free indeed."
John 8:36 NASB

Week 3—Walking in Freedom—Covered 5 Steps:

1 Welcome Home (You are in God's Family)
2 Head (The battle is for the mind)
3 Heart (God's heart is a heart of forgiveness)
4 Hands (We are to serve those around us)
5 What is Your Next Step?

JOURNAL TIME

Jot down areas you continue to struggle with in your faith journey?

Where do you see growth and development in your life right now?

Week 1 Day 3—Review Kingdom Discipleship Part 2 Making Disciples

Part two of Kingdom Discipleship covers the Book of Romans.

Jesus tells us to, "Go Make Disciples of all nations." Matthew 28:19 ESV

The Romans Map serves as our symbol for Part 2—Think of The Romans Map as a globe—to remind you of God's heart for all peoples.

ROMANS MAP

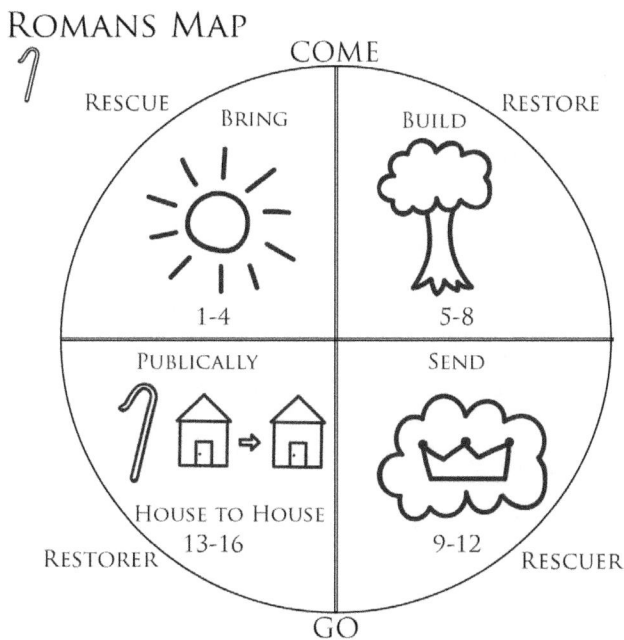

"You will be my witnesses in Jerusalem, and in all Judea and Samaria, and to the end of the earth" **Acts 1:8 (ESV)**

Remember—God desires for you to be fruitful and multiply and fill the earth with the knowledge of his name!

JOURNAL TIME

Reproduce the Romans Map. Where do you see yourself in the book of Romans?

Week 1 Day 4
CORE Discipleship

Jesus, John, Peter, and Paul all model CORE Discipleship.

CORE serves as an acronym for Content, Obedience, Relationship, and Expansion.

CONTENT

Luke opens the book of Acts by talking about "All that Jesus began to do and teach", Acts 1:1 ESV. In Acts 2:42 ESV, Luke says the people "devoted themselves to the apostles' teaching."

Luke's words in Acts remind us of the importance of teaching. Content matters.

OBEDIENCE

Biblical teaching centers of obedience. Look back at Acts 1:1, Jesus did what he taught. Teaching requires action. In Acts 2:42—43, the apostles did . . .

Doing flows out of a heart of obedience to the teaching. Obedience Matters.

RELATIONSHIPS

Acts 2:42, 44-46 speaks of sharing life, sharing food, sharing resources even. Folks met in homes—indicating a relational connection. The early disciples shared their lives with each other. Relationships matter.

EXPANSION

The relational nature of our faith does not mean the focus stays inward. The goal is to reach out and bring more people in—Bring them in. The content, obedience, and relationship build people up, and the inclusion of others occurs as teams are sent out. See Acts 2:41, 47. Expansion matters.

Let's take a closer look at how Jesus modeled CORE Discipleship.

JESUS MODELS CORE DISCIPLESHIP

Content
In the Gospels we see Jesus as a master teacher. Crowds come to hear him, and he instructs them in homes, in the temple, in synagogues, and in the open air gatherings. Jesus utilizes both large and small groups—Publicly and House to House—to get his message across.

Obedience
Jesus expects obedience. He does not teach for content alone. Doing follows knowing. In his last instructions to his followers, he said, "Teach these new disciples to obey all the commands I have given you. And be sure of this: I am with you always, even to the end of the age." **Matthew 28:20 (NLT)**

> "If you keep my commands, you will remain in my love, just as I have kept my Father's commands and remain in his love." **John 15:10 (NIV)**

Relationships

> "While walking by the Sea of Galilee, he saw two brothers, Simon (who is called Peter) and Andrew his brother, casting a net into the sea, for they were fishermen. And he said to them, Follow me, and I will make you fishers of men. Immediately they left their nets and followed him. And going on from there he saw two other brothers, James the son of Zebedee and John his brother, in the boat with Zebedee their father, mending their nets, and he called them. Immediately they left the boat and their father and followed him." **Matthew 4:18-22 (ESV)**

11

Jesus works through relational and social connections. Here are some fun facts.

- Peter and Andrew are brothers.
- James and John are brothers.
- Nathaniel hails from the same town as Peter, Andrew, James, and John.
- Jesus' cousin, John the Baptist, paved the way for his ministry.
- Siblings, Mary, Martha and Lazarus, are among his closest friends.
- When he sends his disciples out on mission, he sends them out by twos.
- Peter, Andrew, James and John are also business partners. See Luke 5:7.

"They signaled to their partners in the other boat to come and help them. And they came and filled both the boats, so that they began to sink." **Luke 5:7 (ESV)**

Go therefore and make disciples of all nations, baptizing them in the name of the Father and of the Son and of the Holy Spirit, teaching them to observe all that I have commanded you. And behold, I am with you always, to the end of the age. **Matthew 28:19-20 (ESV)**

Jesus uses relational language by promising to be "with" them.

Expansion

Jesus tells his disciples to make disciples of "all nations".

"Worthy are you to take the scroll and to open its seals, for you were slain, and by your blood you ransomed people for God from every tribe and language and people and nation, and you have made them a kingdom and priests to our God, and they shall reign on the earth." **Revelation 5:9-10 (ESV)**

Jesus' ministry model includes content, obedience, relationships, and expansion.

John Models CORE Discipleship

"I am writing to you, little children, because your sins are forgiven for his name's sake. I am writing to you, fathers, because you know him who is from the beginning. I am writing to you, young men, because you have overcome the evil one. I write to you, children, because you know the Father. I write to you, fathers, because you know him who is from the beginning. I write to you, young men, because you are strong, and the word of God abides in you, and you have overcome the evil one." **1 John 2:12-14 (ESV)**

Content
Spiritual youth know the word, they grasp basic content.

Obedience
They've overcome the evil one; they fight against sin.

Relationships
Children, youth, fathers, John uses the language of family.

Expansion
John implies reproduction; one can't be a spiritual mother or father without spiritual children.

Peter's Models the CORE Discipleship

Peter models all four requirements of discipleship as well.

Content
Peter pens 1 and 2 Peter as instruction—content. Peter's disciple, John Mark writes our second gospel, the book of Mark. Peter and Mark value content.

Obedience
Peter's two letters make his expectation of obedience clear. John Mark's gospel indicates he follows Peter's commitment of telling others.

Relationships
Peter uses relational language calling John Mark—Mark—his son.

> "She who is at Babylon, who is likewise chosen, sends you greetings, and so does Mark, my son." **1 Peter 5:13 (ESV)**.

Paul informs us Peter, whom he calls Cephas, and the other apostles travel with their wives.

> "Do we not have the right to take along a believing wife, as do the other apostles and the brothers of the Lord and Cephas?" **1 Corinthians 9:6 (ESV)**.

We know early in Jesus' ministry he heals Peter's mother-in-law. Paul informs us of Peter and his wife traveling and ministering together. Peter models ministry including family; the two, ministry and family, need not be in competition.

Expansion
Peter demonstrates an outward focus, expansion, in Acts 1-7, 10.

PAUL MODELS CORE DISCIPLESHIP

Content
Paul expects "the things"—content—he teaches to be passed on.

> "You therefore, my son, be strong in the grace that is in Christ Jesus. The things which you have heard from me in the presence of many witnesses, entrust these to faithful people who will be able to teach others also." **2 Timothy 2:1-2 NASB**

"What you have heard," "teach others also" (ESV), these phrases clearly show the instructional nature of Paul's discipleship.

Obedience
Paul expects his disciples to follow his instruction to teach others.

Part 3: Multiplying Disciples

Relationships
To Timothy, Paul writes, like Peter to Mark, referring to his disciple as his son.

When Paul writes to the Thessalonian church, he emphasizes the relational nature of disciple making.

> "But we were gentle among you, like a nursing mother taking care of her own children. So, being affectionately desirous of you, we were ready to share with you not only the gospel of God but also our own selves, because you had become very dear to us." **1 Thessalonians 2:7-8 (ESV)**

In 1 Thessalonians 2, he speaks of mother, children, brothers, and father, and proceeds to say "imitate" me. Paul's approach to ministry flows relationally.

Expansion
There are four generations represented in 2 Timothy 2:2

- Paul
- Timothy
- The Faithful
- Others

JOURNAL TIME

What content do you believe to be essential for discipling others?

Are you walking in obedience? How so? If not, why not?

Who, in addition to family, do share life with on a weekly basis?

How can you join God in expanding the gospel of the kingdom? Where?

Did you list Kingdom Discipleship as key for discipling others? If so, why? If not, why not?

Week 1 Day 5
The Surrendered Life

In order to join God in what he is doing around the world, we must surrender our lives to him.

God empowers and gifts you, then places you in relationship with others—your spiritual family, your team—so you can tell others of his captivating love (See Acts 1:8).

"And Peter said to them, "Repent and be baptized every one of you in the name of Jesus Christ for the forgiveness of your sins, and you will receive the gift of the Holy Spirit." **Acts 2:38 ESV**

Notice, "The Gift" is God himself—The Holy Spirit.

Read Ephesians 2:8-10
When we surrender our lives to Jesus Christ, the Holy Spirit comes to live inside of us; he is the Gift! We cannot follow Jesus or minister effectively in our own strength. We need him.

It is mentioned in Part 2—Making Disciples—about the famous evangelist of the 19th Century, D. L. Moody, who said he prayed daily to be filled with the Holy Spirit because he leaked. We too need daily filling—for the same reason.

We talk about walking in the Spirit in Part 1—Being a Disciple. Today we focus on surrendering our will to God's will and asking for a fresh filling of the Holy Spirit.

Ephesians 2:10 NASB says,

"For we are His workmanship, created in Christ Jesus for

good works, which God prepared beforehand so that we would walk in them."

The Psalmist expresses a high view regarding individual uniqueness in Psalm 139:13-16 NLT

> [13] "You made all the delicate, inner parts of my body and knit me together in my mother's womb.
> [14] Thank you for making me so wonderfully complex! Your workmanship is marvelous—how well I know it.
> [15] You watched me as I was being formed in utter seclusion, as I was woven together in the dark of the womb.
> [16] You saw me before I was born. Every day of my life was recorded in your book. Every moment was laid out before a single day had passed."

God's design includes your gifting. God put his creativity on display when he made trees, rocks, galaxies, seas, great whites, tigers, elephants, ethnicities, females, males, and you—by the way there are no two "yous".

God uniquely designed you, with skills, gifts, abilities, passions, and desires, for "good works", but to fulfill your divine design, you must yield your will to God's will. God created you to love and enjoy him.

The Father invites you into his divine adventure and empowers you with his Spirit so you can live life to its fullest. When the Father entrusts you with an assignment, he always equips you with all you need to carry it out. **Ministry is a team sport, and God gives each team member, including you, the gifts needed to play the game.**

The first step to being filled with the Holy Spirit is surrender.

Romans 12:1-2 NASB
"Therefore I urge you, brothers *and sisters*, by the mercies of God, to present your bodies as a living and holy sacrifice, acceptable to God, *which is* your spiritual service of worship. [2] And do not be conformed to this world, but be transformed by the renewing of your mind, so that you may prove what the will of God is, that which is good and acceptable and perfect."

The idea of surrender—

Surrender carries with it the idea of subjugation—the laying down of one's will to another. In war, surrender requires giving up or giving in—one army yields territory or relinquishes resistance to the opposing force in hope of gaining life. In ancient times, yielding meant a life of slavery. In marital love, sexual surrender represents yielding to another for mutual pleasure. Surrender to God may resemble more the act of a lover more than the act of a soldier.

Paul reminds us we were enemies of God (Romans 5:10). Perhaps our journey begins by laying down our weapons. The act of surrender may be both/and rather than either/or. God invites us to total surrender; he woos us to come to him. He invites us into a love relationship. Henry Blackaby in his famous work *Experiencing God* points out God's invitation to us is real and personal.

When we surrender to God, we do indeed become his slaves Romans 6. Bob Dylan's song reminds us—"Gotta serve somebody." We either serve sin or we serve righteousness. Slavery to sin results in death, but slavery to righteousness produces a fruitful life. Servitude to God, unlike servitude resulting from an invading army, gives us life, freedom, and abundance.

Here's my prayer of surrender . . .

Father, again I come. I surrender. I lay down my will. I yield my plans, my future, my hopes, and dreams. I come to you not in fear of annihilation, but as a lover coming in vulnerability and full trust. Where does your love want to take us? You are good. You are trustworthy. Your plans are filled with honor and dignity. How do I align my heart with you? I desire to activate the godly desires you place in my heart. I want to chase after you. May lesser things lose their luster. Lover of my soul I want you, nothing else will satisfy, no one else will do, self-serving leaves me empty, Father, I want you. Fill me with your Spirit Holy, Jesus be glorified in my life.

JOURNAL TIME

Take a few moments and write your own prayer of surrender to God. Ask him to fill you with his Holy Spirit afresh and anew.

Take a walk and ask God how he has gifted you, what assignment has he given you?

What steps do you need to take to obey God? Write down details of your experience.

GIFTING AND TEAMS

For the next two weeks, we will explore the topic of spiritual gifts, and ministry teams. How do you discover your spiritual gift(s)? Well, there are several ways. The best way may be to try a lot of different things and discover what you are good at. God often directs our hearts through our interests and desires. God also speaks through others. Ask those who know you best to help you identify your spiritual gifts. No one has all the gifts. There are several lists of spiritual gifts in the Bible. We will explore 1 Peter 4:10-11, Romans 12, 1 Corinthians 12-14, and Ephesians 4. I encourage you to read all of these passages carefully. With a thoughtful reading, you will notice three very important realities.

1 Spiritual gifts always function in the context of **love.**
2 Spiritual gifts never function in isolation, they are always in the context of **relationships**.
3 Spiritual gifts function in public and private contexts (but **homes** show up frequently).

Ephesians 4 provides us with a list of 5 leadership gifts: Apostles, Prophets, Evangelist, Shepherds, and Teachers (APEST). Jesus assumes all five functions in his ministry.

Apostle

"Therefore, holy brothers and sisters, who share in the heavenly calling, fix your thoughts on Jesus, whom we acknowledge as our apostle and high priest." **Hebrews 3:1 NIV**

Prophet

"'Sir', the woman said, 'you must be a prophet.'" **John 4:19 NLT**

Evangelist

In John 4, and in multiple other locations, we see Jesus drawing people to the Father, doing the work of evangelism.

"For the Son of Man came to seek and to save the lost." **Luke 19:10 NIV**

Shepherd

"I am the good shepherd. The good shepherd lays down his life for the sheep." **John 10:11 ESV**

Teacher

"You call Me 'Teacher' and 'Lord'; and you are correct, for *so* I am." **John 13:13 NASB**

In our final week together, we focus on the importance of team ministry. Paul uses the human body to illustrate how spiritual gifts function. The eye needs the ears, the hand needs the foot. Your spiritual gifts come alongside your friends and together others receive the benefit. The same is true with ministry teams. We need others to maximize our effectiveness. God does not typically call lone rangers.

The final day of kingdom discipleship points toward the world. God rescues and restores us, so we can rescue and restore others. God promises us,

"For the earth will be filled With the knowledge of the glory of the Lord, As the waters cover the sea." Habakkuk 2:14 NASB

"Jesus, undeterred, went right ahead and gave his charge: 'God authorized and commanded me to commission you: Go out and train everyone you meet, far and near, in this way of life, marking them by baptism in the threefold name: Father, Son, and Holy Spirit.

PART 3: MULTIPLYING DISCIPLES

Then instruct them in the practice of all I have commanded you. I'll be with you as you do this, day after day after day, right up to the end of the age.'" Matthew 28:18-20 The Message

Let's get started by looking at spiritual gifts.

Week 2: Day 1—The Gift is the Holy Spirit

The God of the Bible is a triune God. Genesis **1:1** and Genesis 1:26 speak of God (The Father) and the Spirit of God. John 1:1-3, 14 and Colossians 1:13-17 tells us even more information about origins; from these passages we learn Jesus was present in creation as well as the Father and Spirit. We also are told in John of God becoming flesh and pitching his tent among us for a short period of time in the life of Jesus (John 1:14). So, from these verses we learn:

God is one, but reveals himself in three persons—God the Father, God the Son, and God the Holy Spirit.

The three in one are eternal, separate from creation, and in perfect fellowship with one another; they live in community.

They, Father, Son, and Spirit invite us into fellowship with them (2 Corinthians 13:14). They say, "Let us create man".

Let's read the verses below to learn more about our triune God—the three in one.

Genesis 1:1-2 NASB
"In the beginning God created the heavens and the earth.
² And the earth was a formless and desolate emptiness, and darkness was over the surface of the deep, and the Spirit of God was hovering over the surface of the waters."

Genesis 1:26 NASB
"Then God said, 'Let Us make mankind in Our image, according to Our likeness; and let them rule over the fish of the sea and over the birds of the sky and over the livestock and over all the earth, and over every crawling thing that crawls on the earth.'"

John 1:1-3 NASB
"In the beginning was the Word, and the Word was with God, and the Word was God. He was in the beginning with God. All things came into being through Him, and apart from Him not even one thing came into being that has come into being."

John 1:14 NASB
"And the Word became flesh, and dwelt among us; and we saw His glory, glory as of the only *Son* from the Father, full of grace and truth."

Colossians 1:13-17 NASB
"For He rescued us from the domain of darkness, and transferred us to the kingdom of His beloved Son, in whom we have redemption, the forgiveness of sins. He is the image of the invisible God, the firstborn of all creation. For by Him all things were created, *both* in the heavens and on earth, visible and invisible, whether thrones or dominions or rulers or authorities—all things have been created through Him and for Him. He is before all things, and in Him all things hold together."

Jesus holds the world together. The Spirit raised Jesus from the dead. The Father and the Son deposited God the Holy Spirit in you when you said yes to Jesus. After the resurrection Jesus told his disciples to go to Jerusalem and wait for the giving of the Holy Spirit. **Acts 2:38 tells us "The Gift" of the Holy Spirit is The Holy Spirit.**

All other gifts come from him. The Holy Spirit is the center of spiritual gifts; he is the source. **God the Holy Spirit dwells inside of you, and what is more The Gift gives gifts.**

The Gift chart below shows an unfolding of gifting from simple to complex.

1
Gifted to
Speak or Serve
2 Pet. 4:10-11

4
Leadership
Gifts
Eph. 4:11

The Gift is
The Holy
Spirit

Acts 2:38

2
Primary
Gifts
Rom. 12:1-13

3
In the
Moment Gifts
*1 Cor. 12:4-11;
12:28*

God gives us himself; he lives within all followers of Jesus—he, God the Holy Spirit, comes to fill, empower, teach, guide, comfort, convict, and lead us.

When I was a teenager, I attended a church for a brief time where they emphasized speaking in tongues as the primary evidence of being filled with the Holy Spirit. They believed "The Gift" was tongues.

However, Paul says at the end of 1 Corinthians 12:30b "Do all speak with tongues?" The Greek construct of the question necessitates the rhetorical response, "NO". A careful reading of Acts 2:38 indicates The Gift is, "The Holy Spirit," not tongues.

In reaction to the teaching of tongues as evidence, many evangelical groups simply reject all teaching on tongues as "dangerous". However, a more balanced approach requires a return to the biblical text.

Since the book of Acts does mention tongues as one of the first gifts given following the outpouring of the Holy Spirit, let's take a closer look at the gift of tongues.

Tongues appears several times in the Bible. There appears to be different expressions—a variety of tongues. Three expressions the New Testament mentions include: a known language, a prayer language, and a message given.

As an understood language (Read Acts 2)

In Acts 2, 120 followers of Jesus speak in tongues, in languages they did not know, and people visiting Jerusalem from around the known world hear the gospel in their own language; 3000 of the hearers become followers of Jesus. The purpose here is clearly evangelism.

My friend Isaac Heath had a similar experience. In his own words,

When I was a teenager, I spent a couple of Summers working with an Inner City missions organization in Chicago called Inner City Impact. In the afternoons, we would go out to do the typical 'evangelism' stuff— basically cold-calling people on the street asking questions like: "If you died tonight, do you know where you would go?" That sort of thing. I was not a fan; but I did it anyway. One afternoon, a friend and I were walking through a park and we came across a young man who was fishing in the park's pond. I don't really know much about fishing, but felt compelled to talk to him. After a few hours, yes hours, of talking to him, he came to accept Christ as his Savior. Needless to say, my friend and I were both ecstatic—after all a young man had come to know Jesus. As we were walking away, my friend casually said, "I didn't know you spoke Spanish." To which I responded, "I don't." She then told me that for the past few hours, I had been speaking fluent Spanish as I talked to this kid. I had no idea. I had been taught that speaking in tongues was not only dangerous, but was probably demonic. Clearly, my mind was changed that day—nothing with a demonic source could have drawn that boy to Christ—it had to have been God, and God alone.

Like in Acts 2, Isaac spoke a language he had not studied resulting in someone coming to know Jesus.

As a prayer language (Read 1 Corinthians 14:14)

Paul says he speaks in tongues more than anyone (1 Corinthians 14:18). He also says when he does so his "mind is unfruitful" (1 Corinthians 14:14). Critics point to the unfruitful statement as "evidence" of tongues being unnecessary; however, to do so takes Paul out of context. Paul, the world's greatest theologian, would not engage in an activity holding no value. He says "now I want all to speak in tongues (1 Corinthians 14:5).

How do we reconcile Paul's apparent contradictions? Private and public use seem to resolve apparent discrepancies. When Paul is spending time in private prayer or singing, he uses tongues as a means of allowing the Spirit of God to speak through him. However, if he gives a message in tongues to a group, he says it needs to be interpreted.

Many times I've been awakened in the middle of night with someone on my mind, frequently one of my children. I've often sensed the Holy Spirit's prompting to pray for the person on my mind. I've frequently been unaware of how or what to pray. During such experiences, I've prayed in tongues until I sensed a release, and then I'd go back to sleep. The next morning, I'd follow up with the individual only to learn they were in some danger, or sick, or seeking God for an answer they received during the night. My mind was unfruitful, but my spirit prayed.

As a message given requiring an interpreter (Read 1 Corinthians 14:27)

The third use, a message given, Paul presents as a public function. Unlike the prayer language, a public address in tongues needs to be interpreted. Why not just give the message in the language of the speaker? When a person speaks a prophecy, the speaker addresses the hearer and two people get blessed. However, when a message is given in tongues, and an interpreter responds, the speaker, the interpreter, and the audience, all receive the blessing—God loves using teams by involving more people.

JOURNAL TIME

Read 2 Corinthians 13:14. Jot down your observations.

Did you notice the trinity in this verse? God the Father, God the Son, and God the Holy Spirit are all present. Paul highlights Jesus' grace, the Father's love, and the Holy Spirit's fellowship. The word fellowship at its core means "shared life". The Holy Spirit wants the intimacy of sharing his life with you, and he wants you to share your life with him. In Romans, Paul talked about walking in the Spirit in Romans 8. Walking together enables us to share life.

In what ways have you experienced God the Holy Spirit?

Take a walk and share your joy, sorry, dreams, fears—your life with God the Holy Spirit. After you walk, write about your experience.

Week 2: Day 2
Gifted to Speak or Serve

1
Gifted to
Speak or Serve
2 Pet. 4:10-11

The Gift is
The Holy
Spirit

Acts 2:38

4
Leadership
Gifts
Eph. 4:11

2
Primary
Gifts
Rom. 12:1-13

3
In the
Moment Gifts
*1 Cor. 12:4-11;
12:28*

Gifted to Speak or Serve—Read 1 Peter 4:10-11

The Gift, the Holy Spirit, gives gifts. Peter says everyone has "a gift"
(1 Peter 4:10, 1 Corinthians 12:7). There is no such thing as an
ungifted follower of Jesus Christ. God gifts his kids. On the one
hand, God chooses (1 Cor. 12:11), and on the other, he tells us to ask
(James 4:2, 1 Corinthians 14:1). We may ask God for any gift, but he
chooses.

People tend to lean toward being either introverted or
extraverted. Ruth Brannen joined our church planting team when

she was 75. She took several spiritual gift inventories. However, she remained confused about her gifting. One day, I sat down with her in her den and I opened my Bible to 1 Peter 4:10-11. I read the passage and asked Ruth, do you prefer "speaking or being behind the scenes serving". She scoffed, and said, "You know the answer to that." Ruth clearly demonstrated a servant's heart. She would be terrified if I ever asked her to come up front and speak. From then on, she knew her gift; she was a servant.

With many of the gifts, there are corresponding roles. Roles are not gifts, but they are important. All followers of Jesus are called to serve, to give, to show mercy, to offer hospitality, to share their faith, and so forth. However, there are those who are gifted in these things; they are motivated by their gifting—this was true of Ruth—the servant.

1 Peter 4:10-11 provides us with the simplest gift list in the Bible. Next week we will look at primary gifts, situational gifts, leadership gifts, gift clusters, and discuss how your gifts help in the formation and function of team development.

JOURNAL TIME

Do you prefer to speak or serve, be upfront and seen, or are you a behind the scene kind of person?

Write out an example.

Share with your discipleship partner your responses.

WEEK 2 DAY 3
PRIMARY GIFTS

1
Gifted to
Speak or Serve
2 Pet. 4:10-11

4
Leadership
Gifts
Eph. 4:11

The Gift is
The Holy
Spirit

Acts 2:38

2
Primary
Gifts
Rom. 12:1-13

3
In the
Moment Gifts
*1 Cor. 12:4-11;
12:28*

Primary Gifts—Read Romans 12:1-13

Paul gives a list of seven gifts in Romans 12: Prophecy, Service, Teaching, Encouraging, Giving, Leadership, and Mercy. Some writers refer to these seven as motivational gifts; I call them primary gifts. These gifts tend to be steering gifts. When you wake up in the morning, you simply find yourself doing these things out of an intrinsic motivation. They function at a primal level.

When I was 18, I visited my sister Carrie in Asheboro, NC. She encouraged me to attend a Bible study with a group of kids my age. I showed up at the house and Don Bulla answered the door. He asked my name. I said, "Doug Dorman", and he said, "Dorman, you will open doors for people to the gospel; you are a teacher." All I said was my name. Don's prophetic word—a primary gift for him, called out "teacher" a primary gift for me. His words affirmed my thoughts and desires.

Romans 12 gifts tend to be life-long deposits; I see the world through a teacher's eyes. However, with maturity our gifts may cluster with additional gifts such as tongues, or evangelism.

JOURNAL TIME

Read Romans 12: 1-13.

When you look at the list, does one gift stand out?

Write about how you have exercised one of the gifts found in this section of scripture.

Ask your discipleship partner what they see in your life. Ask them, "what gift from Romans 12 do you see in my life?" Then discuss this together and pray for each other. Write about the experience.

Week 2 Day 4
"In the Moment" Gifts

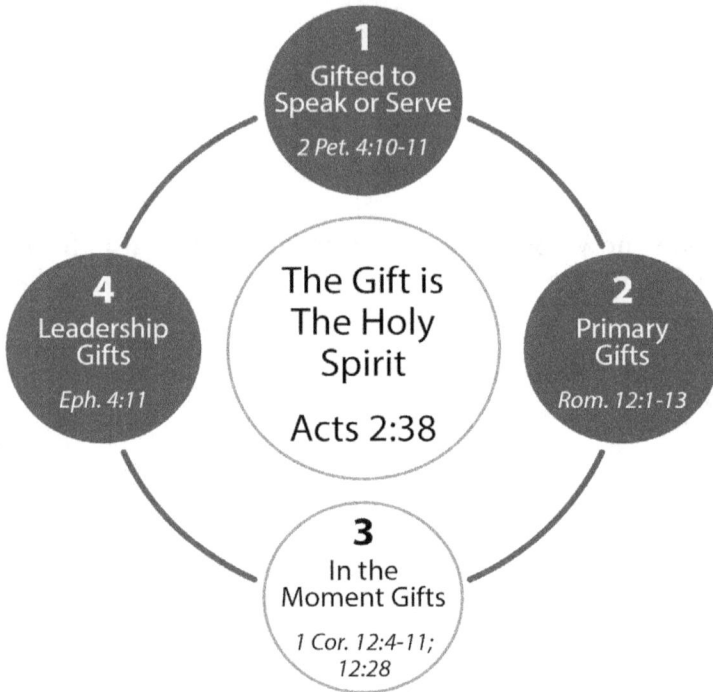

```
                    ┌─────────────┐
                    │      1      │
                    │  Gifted to  │
                    │Speak or Serve│
                    │ 2 Pet. 4:10-11│
                    └─────────────┘

┌─────────────┐   ┌─────────────┐   ┌─────────────┐
│      4      │   │ The Gift is │   │      2      │
│ Leadership  │   │  The Holy   │   │   Primary   │
│   Gifts     │   │   Spirit    │   │    Gifts    │
│  Eph. 4:11  │   │  Acts 2:38  │   │ Rom. 12:1-13│
└─────────────┘   └─────────────┘   └─────────────┘

                    ┌─────────────┐
                    │      3      │
                    │   In the    │
                    │ Moment Gifts│
                    │ 1 Cor. 12:4-11;│
                    │    12:28    │
                    └─────────────┘
```

"In the Moment" Gifts—Read 1 Corinthians 12:4-11; 12:28

Unlike primary gifts, "in the moment" gifts tend to come and go; although, there are those who flow in these giftings more frequently than others. In the first part of the chapter, Paul outlines nine gifts. Some refer to these as sign gifts. John Wimber, leader of the Vineyard Movement preferred the term "situational gifts"; I call them "In the moment" gifts. These gifts occur based on the prompting of the Holy Spirit "in the moment."

For example, healing is not my primary gifting. However, I prayed for a man in our church who was partially deaf. On his ride home following the service, he and his wife rolled the windows down because it was a nice spring day. While sitting at a traffic light, he said to his wife, "Isn't the singing of the birds beautiful." She later wrote to me and told me of the healing, explaining, "He'd not been able to hear birds for years."

I love when the Holy Spirit provides gifting "in the moment". I've also prayed for folks who have died. So, you might want someone else to pray for you who has a more consistent track record.

JOURNAL TIME

Read over 1 Corinthians 12:4-11.

On the nine gifts mentioned, have you experienced any "in the moment" gifting?

Is there a current situation in your life, where you need one of these nine gifts? Ask the Holy Spirit to empower you to meet the need.

WEEK 2 DAY 5
LEADERSHIP GIFTS

1
Gifted to
Speak or Serve
2 Pet. 4:10-11

4
Leadership
Gifts
Eph. 4:11

The Gift is
The Holy
Spirit

Acts 2:38

2
Primary
Gifts
Rom. 12:1-13

3
In the
Moment Gifts
*1 Cor. 12:4-11;
12:28*

Last week we introduced spiritual gifts. We said, The Gift is The Holy Spirit. We also said, he gives gifts to us. To review:

- You are gifted to speak or serve (Upfront or Behind the scenes wiring) 2 Peter 4:10-11
- You have a primary gift Romans 12:1-13
- You may experience "in the moment" gifts 1 Corinthians 12:4-11, 12:28

Now, we turn to Leadership gifts and gift pairing or clustering.

Leadership Gifts—Ephesians 4:11

The second half of 1 Corinthians 12 mentions several gifts we find repeated in other places. The exceptions include the gift of helps and the gift of administration. Perhaps administration would be better translated as leadership. The word refers to a pilot of a ship. The job of the pilot was to meet a ship coming from the sea and pilot the ship up the river avoiding the shoals. For these reasons, the New American Standard Bible links the word pilot as a synonym with leadership in Romans 12:8.

Several New Testament passages speak about leadership gifts. Look up the following passages in your Bible.
- Hebrews 13:7, 17 Leaders ἡγουμένων, (ēgoumenōn).
- Romans 12:8 Leadership προϊστάμενος (proistamenos)— Visionary leaders
- (create or recognize opportunities others may not think of or believe to be possible).
- 1 Corinthians 12:28 Administration κυβέρνησις (kybernesis)— Solves problems—like a pilot on a ship.
- Ephesians 4:11-12 Apostles, Prophets, Evangelist, Shepherds, and Teachers—APEST.

Other types of leaders mentioned in the New Testament include:

Deacons (Servants) Bishops and Elders. It appears bishops, elders and shepherds function the same ; the words are synonyms. Acts 20:17, 28; 1 Peter 5:1-5. Regardless of title, the Bible emphasizes humility and an attitude of service.

Read Ephesians 4: 11-12 APEST Leaders
- Apostles
- Prophets
- Evangelists
- Shepherds
- Teachers

Perhaps these are expressions of the Leadership gift mentioned in Romans 12:8. The writer of Hebrews seems to be referring to this in Hebrews 13:7, 17 where he simply uses a generic term "leader" without reference to titles.

Function is more important than form or title.

Leadership Qualifications

Read 1 Timothy 3:1-13 and Titus 1:5-9

Those with leadership gifts tend to have pairing gifts or a cluster of gifts—They frequently operate with a variety of gifts. The gifts strengthen and support one another—as in Acts 2 with tongues and evangelism. My primary gift of teaching frequently pairs or clusters with knowledge and wisdom. Robert Clinton, author of *The Making of a Leader*, calls the pairing of gifts, "gift clusters". Leaders tend to be multi-gifted. Leaders typically have a primary gift (what they are passionate about—they wake up excited about their primary gifting). Those with a leadership gift often have a gift of faith which enables them to step out and take calculated risks.

JOURNAL TIME

To discover your passion ask yourself, "What am I excited about?" Then look over the various passages on spiritual gifts and ask, "What gifts do I need to live out my passion?

What have others said you are good at?

Where do you see spiritual fruit?

Can you identify your primary gift?

What are your support gifts? How do your primary and support gifts work together? Talk these things over with your disciple partner this week.

Week 3 Day 1
Relational and Missional

For my dissertation, I interviewed 32 individuals on eight teams from four different Cross-cultural ministries in order to better understand how teams formed and functioned.[1] The data revealed not only how teams came together and operated, but also how teams dealt with conflict and how teams multiplied. I dubbed the eight teams, Mobile Apostolic Training Teams (MATTs). The rest of the week we will unpack the findings of the MATTs research.

MATTS form, function, deal with conflict, and multiply by navigating the dynamic tension between being both relational and missional. Paul provides an excellent model of one living in relationships and on mission. Paul mentions his partners by name in each of his letters. He uses familial language, showing us his relational side. In 1 Thessalonians 2—in verse 7 he refers to himself as a nursing mother, and in verse 11 calls himself a father. He calls Timothy his son in 2 Timothy 1:1.

Paul's missional commitment manifests throughout the book of Acts. In chapter 13, the Antioch church sends Barnabas and Paul on

---

[1] Dorman, Lloyd Douglas, (2019). *The Formation and Function of Mobile Apostolic Training Teams in Multiplying Churches.* ProQuest.

mission. The word apostle means "one sent". In Latin the word apostle translates as "missionary". Paul makes three cross-cultural journeys, and he always seeks to take the message to those who have not yet heard. Paul's teams grow in size and impact on each successive trip.

The eight teams I studied were also apostolic. They "were sent" internationally to train disciples, leaders, and churches, to multiply movements around the world.

See the following two charts to understand Paul's commitment to relational ministry and numeric growth.

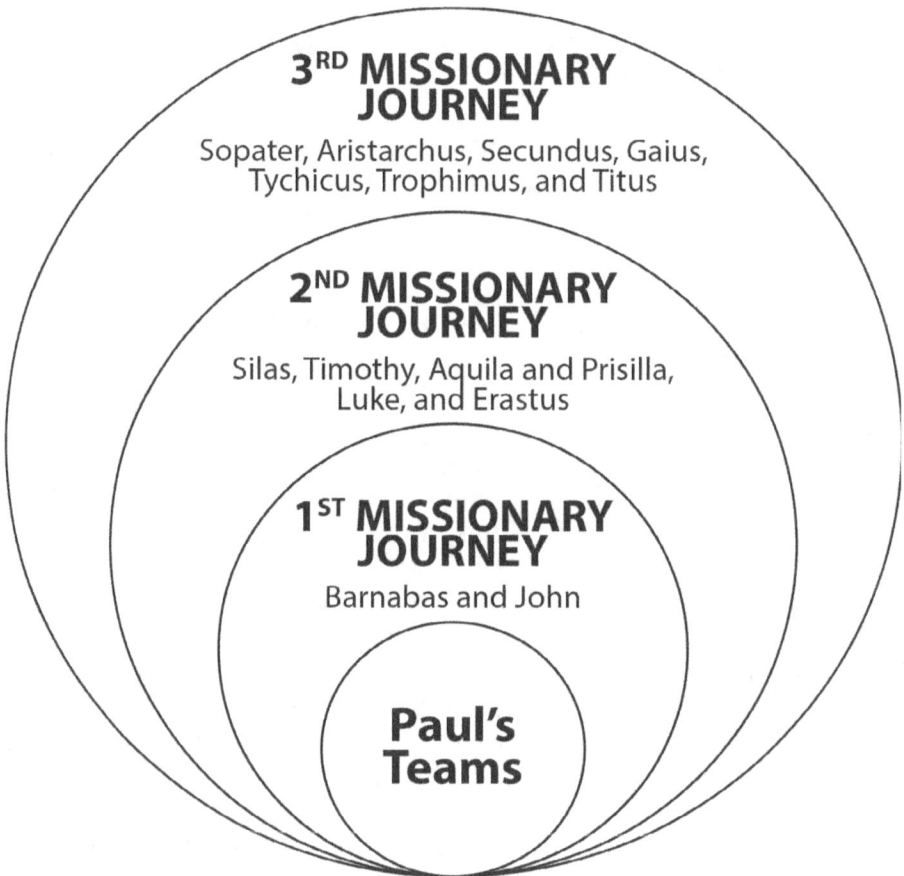

3RD MISSIONARY JOURNEY

Sopater, Aristarchus, Secundus, Gaius, Tychicus, Trophimus, and Titus

2ND MISSIONARY JOURNEY

Silas, Timothy, Aquila and Prisilla, Luke, and Erastus

1ST MISSIONARY JOURNEY

Barnabas and John

Paul's Teams

TABLE 1. EXPANDED CHART OF PAUL'S APOSTOLIC TRAINING TEAM MEMBERS.

MEMBER	PASSAGE	MEMBER	PASSAGE	MEMBER	PASSAGE
Barnabas	Acts 4:36	Sopater	Acts 20:4	Jesus Justus	Col 4:11
John Mark	Acts 12:23	Urbanus	Rom 16:9	Demas	Col 4:14
Silas	Acts 15:12	Stephanas	1 Cor 1:16 16:17	Luke	Col 4:14
Timothy	Acts 16:1	Achaicus	1 Cor 16:17	Phygellus	2 Tim 1:15
Aquilla	Acts 18:2	Fortunatus	1 Cor 16:17	Hermogenes	2 Tim 1:15
Pricilla	Acts 18:2	Silvanus (Same as Silas?)	2 Cor 1:19 Acts 17:14-15	Onesiphorus	2 Tim 1:16
Sosthenes	Acts 18:17	Titus	2 Cor 2:13	Crescens	2 Tim 4:10
Aristarchus	Acts 19:29	Epaphroditus	Phil 2:25	Carpus	2 Tim 4:13
Gaius	Acts 19:29	Syntyche	Phil 4:2	Claudia	2 Tim 4:21
Trophimus	Acts 20:4	Clement	Phil 4:3	Pudens	2 Tim 4:21
Tychicus	Acts 20:4	Epaphras	Col 1:17	Aretemas	Titus 3:12
				LINUS	2 Tim 4:21

(Morris & Graf, 2013, p. 128)

45

Let's take a closer look at:
- How Teams Form
- How Teams Function
- How Teams Deal with Conflict
- How Teams Multiply

The seesaw diagram shows the balance between relationships and mission. Notice both the "Relationships" box and the "Mission" box contain the same four words: Formation, Function, Conflict, and Multiply.

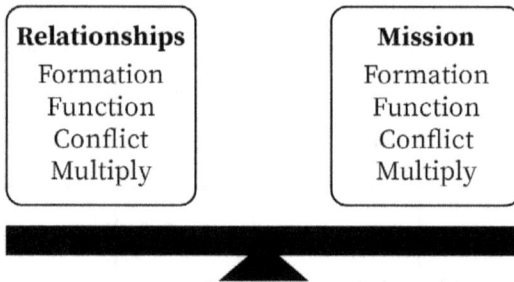

Relationships	**Mission**
Formation	Formation
Function	Function
Conflict	Conflict
Multiply	Multiply

When teams only focus on relationships, they settle for the familiar and eventually implode. However, when teams commit to mission alone, they inevitably explode. Task driven teams tend to use people to accomplish the mission. Leadership requires balancing the tension by being both relational and missional in all aspects—how they form, function, address conflict, and multiply.

Paul says in Romans 12 the church resembles the human body. Each member functions interdependently. The body of Jesus Christ, the church, operates with a relational commitment and a missional focus. Like the human body the church's mission expresses life through the connections of the parts. Love guides the interaction of each member.

My wife, Joan, is a nurse. Our daughter, Charis, and son, Ian, are following in their mom's footsteps. Charis is in her last year of nursing school, and Ian is in his first year of med school. Our dinner discussions occasionally turn to the intricacies of the human body's design. If Joan, Charis, or Ian go into too much detail, I redirect the conversation, so I don't pass out. However, even I find the various systems of the body fascinating. The respiratory, circulatory, nervous, and the reproductive system work synergistically. In a similar way MATTs form, function, navigate conflict, and multiply through systems enabling the body of Christ to impact the world.

**MATTs Form and Function
with a Dynamic Tension Between
Relationships and Mission**

Formation		Function
Attracted • To Relationships • To the Mission	**Recruited** • Gifts • Skills • Integrity • Experience	**8 Ways** • Build Relationally • Encourage and Empower Nationals • Support One Another • Train Pastors, Leaders, and Church Planters • Take Risks • Evangelize • Announce the Kingdom • Multiply
Conflict		**Multiplication**
• Use the Bible • Use Psychology and Cultural Sensitivity • Use Business Practices • Use Wisdom		• Complete Training Cycle • Pass the Baton

The remainder of our study will unpack how:
- The respiratory system forms,
- The circulatory functions,
- The nervous system navigates conflict,
- The reproductive system multiplies
- Each of the four systems balance the dynamic tension between being relational and missional.

JOURNAL TIME

Today we introduced several charts. Take some time and look back over each chart.

Write down questions you have about each chart.

List at least two observations about each chart.

Week 3 Day 2:
The Respiratory System:
How Teams Form

MATTs inhale and exhale through attraction and recruitment.

The Holy Spirit designs gifts to be exercised in teams. Your gifts require other gifts to function properly. Teams are needed locally, regionally, and globally, to empower the church to bring the lost in, build the saved up, and send the body out.

When building ministry teams, the following six items really matter.

1. Character Matters
We've all seen extremely gifted individuals crash and burn, because their gifting exceeded their character, and they operated as lone rangers.

2. Skills Matter
Teams need people on them who bring abilities to the table. Good music, quality financial practices, and expert organization make good teams better.

3. Gifting Matters
If you send out a teaching team, you need teachers on the team; if you send out service teams, having someone who knows which end of the hammer to use proves useful.

4. Emotional Health Matters
Teams need emotionally healthy team members. Test volunteers in local contexts before releasing them into a global context. Help them

process hurts, habits, and hang-ups, see week three of **Kingdom Discipleship—Part 1—Being a Disciple**? Before you build a team, look for people who are growing, moving toward Jesus.

5. Humility Matters
Prideful people may be gifted and skilled, but they will hinder a team's ability to serve and minister.

. Compatibility Matters
You want people who get along well with each other. Can they laugh together, cry together, and serve one another?

To summarize where we have been and where we are going; the goal is multiplication. The church must be about the business of multiplying disciples, leaders, churches, and movements. Leadership is required to grow churches, and leadership needs to function through gifted teams.

There are three types of leaders worth mentioning.
1 Local leaders
2 Regional leaders
3 Global leaders

Paul and Peter set up **local leaders** within churches . . . they were to shepherd the flock
Acts 20:17-38
1 Peter 5:1-5
Regional leaders train outside of their local areas, the entire book of Acts is filled with these types of examples. **They serve trans-locally.**
Acts 1:8 gives us the template of moving from local to global.
Paul was a **global leader**—his ministry expanded beyond local and regional influence. His writings impact us today.
Acts 9:15-16 reveals Paul's calling to ministry to leaders, Jews, and Gentiles—three audiences.
Romans 12:8 speaks of a gift of leadership
1 Corinthians 12:28 speaks of a navigating gift (administration)
Ephesians 4:11-16 outlines different expressions of leadership
Paul rarely traveled alone. In all of his epistles, he states his

name in the opening verse or verses. He includes fellow workers in his opening sentences. Some exceptions apply. Romans, Galatians, Ephesians, 1 and 2 Timothy, and Titus. These books simply have Paul's name in the opening verse. However, this is only if one does a surface reading.

Romans closes with a list of leaders

Paul's travel in Galatia found in Acts reveals additional team members

In Ephesians, Paul closes by mentioning Tychicus

In 1 and 2 Timothy and Titus, the letters are written to apostolic team members

Attraction

Robert Clinton in his book, *The Making of a Leader* speaks of those with like gifts gravitate toward one another. Individuals join teams because they feel attracted to the leader, or the leader feels attracted toward them.

During high school and college, I sought mentors who challenged and helped me grow intellectually and spiritually. Mrs. Southern, who was close to my mom's age, served as a spiritual mother. She encouraged me to never settle for less than God's best for my life. She pushed me toward holy living and never tolerated foolish jesting. On one occasion I visited Mrs. Southern at her house and she asked me what I had been up to. I joked saying I'd been out getting drunk. She did not see humor in my statement and sternly admonished me to not speak flippantly about worldly living. I've tried to speak more soberly since. Mrs. Southern gave me books to read, tapes to listen to, and magazines to consume. She encouraged me to attend conferences, Bible studies, and seek my parents input on my decisions. She critiqued messages I gave and edited my poor grammar. She pushed me to pursue excellence and to gain more education.

Dr. Ron Lackey taught religion at Coastal Carolina University.[2] He introduced me to a new dimension of academia. He encouraged me to read more broadly, think more deeply, wrestle with my doubts, and dream big dreams. He served as a spiritual father to me. One of his class assignments required each student to give a

---

[2] In 1981-83, it was Coastal Carolina College.

presentation on a passage of scripture. I chose to give an overview of a section of Romans. Back in his office we debriefed my delivery. He said my tone came across as harsh and uninviting. He suggested speaking more slowly, looking people in the eye, and giving more examples. Even when he corrected me, Dr. Lackey embodied encouragement. I did not feel rebuked; I felt a desire to improve.

My desire to pursue a PhD, to teach, to mentor, to push others toward maturity can be traced back to time in Dr. Lackey's office, home, and lunches at the cafeteria. Jeff Dunn and I once helped him move into a new home; he had lots of books. I slipped into his classroom once after transferring to Asbury University.[3] He was showing a film on the life of Dietrich Bonhoeffer. When the film finished, he introduced me to his class calling me an unorthodox thinker and a diligent student.[4]

Both Mrs. Southern and Ron Lackey possessed qualities I admired: they taught with passion; their instruction flowed from who they were not just what they said. They embodied their convictions, insights, and knowledge and shared freely with the curious. They both demonstrated love and care. Mrs. Southern and Dr. Lackey loomed as giants in my eyes, but they quickly sought to minimize their stature and maximize mine. They became more than tutors; they became friends. I desired to be like them decades ago; I still do.

Today I serve as a mentor for others. Those who seek to spend time with me typically have gifts and qualities I hold in a more advanced form. I think back to Mrs. Southern and Dr. Lackey and seek to immolate their style by asking questions, praising strengths, pointing out weaknesses gently, and connecting them with human and verbalized (print, video, audio) resources to help them grow. I also seek to move the relationship toward friendship quickly by including mentees as co-trainers with me on teams. MATTs develop out of mentoring relationships. Friends form teams.

When I was growing up, the kids in the neighborhood gathered on the corner of 74th Avenue North and Ocean Boulevard to decide if we were going to play football, baseball, kick the can, or basketball.

---

[3] In 1983-1985, it was Asbury College.

[4] By caalling me unorthodox, Dr. Lackey was not referring to my theology, but to my practice of seeking unconventional answers and not simply being satisfied with the status quo.

If a team was involved, Charles was the captain. I always wanted to be on Charles' team, because his team won.

MATTs are a lot like our crew on 74th Ave. Team members are not strangers, they know each other. Often members point back to serving together in college ministries or on church staffs. Hearing MATTs tell their stories carry the feel of, "The time Charles threw me the pass, and I ran for the winning touchdown."

Like kids playing pickup games in the a vacant lot, MATTs want to win. They want to know their team makes a difference. Relationships matter on teams. Choosing relationships with history to them increases the impact because the players know who can catch the ball, run the ball, or block the opponents.

A few years back a friend and his son joined me on a trip to Zambia. He said yes to my invitation, because he desired for the three of us to spend time together. He added, "I've always wanted to go to Africa." My friend was attracted both to the relationship and the mission. I found several of those who joined MATTs felt a draw not only to the team members but also to the location of the training.

Recruitment
When Charles selected a team in our neighborhood, he did so with precision. He wanted to be sure to have players who knew when to shoot, when to throw the ball, how to catch, how to block, how to play as a team, and how to follow his lead. His goal was clear—win the game.

Mobile apostolic leaders recruit team members in a similar way. They pick players who's gifts, skills, integrity, and experience enable them to work compatibly together. Gifts of teaching, encouragement, service, healing, administration, and prophecy surface regularly. Leaders select people with logistical abilities and interpersonal skills. Marital faithfulness, financial responsibility, and humility are prerequisites; leaders repeatedly emphasize the importance of integrity when building a team. Team leaders seek recruits with a proven ministry track record and hopefully some international experience. On occasion they select members who lack passport experience, but who carry local or regional influence.

JOURNAL TIME

Character, skills, gifting, compatibility, emotional health, humility, and compatibility were six things listed as mattering. Where do you desire to grow? Pick one or two and write your thoughts. Perhaps process what you write with someone you trust.

Who has served as a mentor in your life?

What did you learn from them?

Think back to teams you have been on. What role did attraction play?

How were you recruited?

Why were you recruited?

Week 3 Day 3:
The Circulatory System: How Teams Function

The BEST TEAM Model—8 Characteristics of Mobile Apostolic Training Teams (MATTs)
- **B**uild Relationally—Healthy teams build relationally.
- **E**ncourage and Empower Nationals
- **S**upport One Another
- **T**rain Pastors, Leaders and Church Planters
- **T**ake Risk
- **E**vangelize
- **A**nnounce the Kingdom
- **M**ultiply

BEST TEAMs

The first four characteristics are **relational**, and the second four are **missional**!

Teams need to be both relational and missional.

Action attracts leaders. Teams form, not to stay in the huddle, but to play ball. What causes leaders' hearts to beat and blood to flow is how well a team functions on the field. MATTs flow in eight exciting ways. These eight functions divide nicely into four relational functions and four missional functions. Together the eight elements provide us with the acronym—BEST TEAMs.

The four relational elements include:
- **B**uilding relationally,
- **E**ncouraging and empowering nationals,
- **S**upporting one another,
- **T**raining pastors, leaders, and church planters

The more missional elements include:
- **T**aking risks,
- **E**vangelizing,
- **A**nnouncing the kingdom,
- **M**ultiplying

Let's look at the BEST elements a bit more closely.

Build Relationally

Teams do not usually form randomly. Leaders and members come together who know each other; they share past experiences. Formation goes beyond simply being relational or friendly, MATTs sovereignly share history together. They express feeling a connection, a bond. Some members see their relationships as part of their calling. Paul Petrie says it this way, "Destiny is a corporate matter, once we discover the people with whom our destiny lies, the rest will unfold."

Encourage and Empower Nationals

Team members seek not only to teach and train but to encourage and empower national leaders. Trainers commit to sitting with, walking with, talking with, and most importantly listening to the national leaders. The time together is not simply content driven. The relationships, the friendships, matter. Trainers show genuine interest in participants families, challenges, and dreams.

Support One Another

Team members tend to be involved in each other's lives on and off the court. They follow up with each other between trips. They discuss family problems, personal struggles, ministry disappoints, setbacks, advances, victories, and desires. They know the families of their team. MATTs come alongside each other in meaningful ways, relational ways. When not traveling together, team members spend time together; they just hang out—eating together, sharing a cup of coffee, surfing, playing tennis, or planning for the next trip.

Train pastors, leaders, and church planters

At first glance, training seems like a missional element. Indeed it can be and often is. But, as the teams describe their interactions with trainees, it quickly becomes apparent a relational dimension permeates the training sessions. The training carries a more intimate family feel than a class room ethos. Small group interaction and discussions around meals is an integral part of the training.

Now let's turn our attention to the four missional, TEAM, qualities of MATTs.

Take Risk

Teams take risks in order to fulfill their mission. All eight teams speak of some form of physical risk occurring during their cross-cultural adventures. Malaria, Covid-19, and other health risks exist. All eight teams also refer to demonic, governmental, or dangers from robbers, gangs, militia, etc. Like special ops teams, MATTs make exfil plans. All MATTs rely heavily on local leadership to minimize risks and maximize safety.

MATTs ask questions:
- Where is the embassy in relationship to where we are training?
- What are our exit routes?
- How do we communicate if we get separated?
- Do we need members on this trip who have military training— who know how to navigate a dicey situation and safely evacuate the team?

Evangelizing
MATTs share their faith with the not yet convinced. All eight teams teach on evangelism and several implement their training in real time—sending out team members to share their faith immediately after instruction. The trainees report back on their experiences.

In Zambia and Tanzania, our team sent out pastors two by two to share the Tree Trees illustration mentioned in **Kingdom Discipleship Part 1—Being a Disciple**. Each time we sent folks out, people came to faith in Jesus Christ. In both countries, pastors were not comfortable sharing their faith directly—they grew up in church cultures where sharing the gospel of the kingdom was a pulpit function. However, seeing the results broadened these pastors' perspectives.

Announcing the Kingdom
MATTs do not build the kingdom; they seek and announce the kingdom. God expands the kingdom and builds the church. MATTs understand the kingdom to be already available and not yet complete. New Testament scholar George Ladd and apostolic pioneer John Wimber both extrapolate on announcing the already and the not yet of the kingdom of God.[5] The kingdom's advance includes signs and wonders. All eight teams report stories of healing, deliverance, directional dreams, visions, giving and receiving prophetic words.

In the gospels, Jesus uses signs and wonders to show the Father's love, overcome the evil one, and show compassion. In the book of Acts, signs and wonders follow the announcement of the kingdom. Paul's frequently refers to the power of the Holy Spirit in his letters and affirms the accompaniment of signs and wonders

---

[5] Leader with the Vineyard Movement.

when the kingdom is declared. Since Jesus remains the same, MATTs see their ministry as a continuation of the words and works of Jesus.

Hebrews 13:8, NASB
"Jesus Christ is the same yesterday and today, and forever."

Multiply
MATTs are not content with simply delivering a series of lectures and then moving on. Each team makes a two to three year commitment to the group they train. They expect trainees to carry the training yet further. Those trained train others who train still others.

JOURNAL TIME

Read Ephesians 4. In what way do you see BEST TEAM practices in the passage?

Write about a time you were part of a team.

What part did you play?

What went well?

What did not go so well?

What gifts do you bring to a ministry team?

Week 3 Day 4:
The Nervous System
How Teams Deal with Conflict

Mobile Apostolic Training Teams (MATTs) cross borders to plant new faith communities locally, regionally, and globally. They balance tension between remaining relational and missional. However, healthy teams also experience conflict.

Relational Conflict—Things were going so well—And Then

> **Psalm 133:1 ESV**
> "Behold, how good and pleasant it is when brothers dwell in unity!"

Paul's first missionary team fell apart due to conflict.

Good Times—Barnabas and Saul (Paul)
Acts 9:26-30 . . . **But Barnabas**, Acts 11:24-26, Acts 13:1-3
Paul and Barnabas, started out as Barnabas and Paul in the verses above, the shift occurs in Acts 13:4-13, 16. They successfully fulfill the missional side of the equation and return with great reports of what God did.

Paul rises in leadership—Paul and Barnabas
Acts 13:4-13, 16 . . . **Now Paul**
However, during the first trip, Barnabas' cousin, John Mark (Who Peter refers to as my son) bails half way through the trip (Perhaps when Paul becomes the leader and not his cousin).

Conflict results—between friends
Acts 15:36-41

When planning for the second trip, Barnabas wants to bring John Mark along, but Paul says nothing doing, pointing out he quit on midway through the last trip. [6] Paul and Barnabas get in a big fight over who to take on a team. They can't come to an agreement so they agree to disagree and form two teams—Barnabas take Mark, and Paul takes Silas, and later adds a new guy, Timothy.

Acts 15:39-40 NASB
"Now it turned into such a sharp disagreement that they separated from one another, and Barnabas took Mark with him and sailed away to Cyprus. But Paul chose Silas, and left after being entrusted by the brothers to the grace of the Lord."

It seems Paul goes where he started churches before his work in Antioch. See Acts 15:16 where Luke speaks of Cilicia, the province where Tarsus was. He strengthens the churches there. In Galatians 1, Paul mentions Syria and Cilia. About 11 years pass between Galatians 1:18 and Galatians 1:23; the believers seem to have formed into churches, see Acts 15:41, and Paul and Silas arrive to strengthen these followers of Jesus.[7]

The Rest of the Story—Equals
Philemon 1:24	Fellow Worker
2 Timothy 4:11	Very Useful
1 Peter 5:13	My Son

However, the split does not mark the end of the story. Barnabas, who originally mentored Paul, continues to operate in his mentoring role with his cousin, Mark. After some time, Mark matures and Paul mellows. Paul, in his final letter, requests to see Mark, adding a statement of his value.

---

[6] In Acts 13, Mark is called John. The New Living Translation inserts John Mark in Acts 13 in an attempt to clarify who John is.

[7] From personal correspondence with Dr. Linus Morris on Tuesday, 26 October 2021.

2 Timothy 4:11 NASB
"Only Luke is with me. Pick up Mark and bring him with you, for he is useful to me for service."

Although scripture does not tell us when or how reconciliation occurred between Paul and Mark, evidently hearts changed. We should be thankful Barnabas did not give up on his cousin; if he had, perhaps we'd not have the gospel written by Mark's hand in our biblical text.

Conflict makes us nervous. However, the nervous system is part of how the body works. MATTs see conflict as normative. My friend Linus Morris builds in a conflict management piece in his training. At the end of each days' training, the team debriefs using the WIN exercise—

- What went **w**ell?
- What do we need to **i**mprove?
- What do we need to do **n**ext?

Conflict happens. Not being surprised by it allows teams to process conflict in healthy ways. The WIN exercise is not always comfortable. In South America a team member interrupted me during my session, and I became annoyed. He stepped toward the stage to explain the material more clearly than he thought I was doing. As he approached the stage, I balled up my fist, looked him in the eye, and said, "Not now." I continued to teach, and he sat down.

During our WIN exercise, our conflict came up. I apologized for being angry, defensive, and ready to punch him. He apologized for trying to take over my time. He also admitted I made the points he was afraid I was going to leave out. If we left the situation unattended, our friendship would have ruptured and the team's mission would have been hindered. By seeing conflict as normative and welcoming processing, teams grow.

Use the Bible
In Matthew 18 Jesus addresses how to negotiate when offenses occur. Jesus informs us to go to the person directly. If the offender refuses to receive one on one instruction, take a second person along. Where two or three are present, Jesus promises to show up.

Matthew 18:20 NASB
"For where two or three have gathered together in My name,
I am there in their midst."

Jesus' words in Matthew 18, and Paul's experience with Mark show us the biblical example is to seek restoration of relationships when they get strained. All healthy teams experience conflict. In addition to using the Bible as our template for reconciliation, MATTs also utilize tools from business, psychology, and Holy Spirit applied wisdom.

Business
The return to a biblical center restores relationships and encourages members to get back in the game, back on task. Team members also utilize business resources to help teams stay on course—three resources come to mind:
- *The Five Dysfunctions of a Team,* by Patrick Lencioni's,
- *Built to Last,* by Jim Collins and Jerry L. Porras,
- *Good to Great* by Jim Collins

Business principles and practices prove helpful to get teams back on track during times of distraction or conflict. Business writings nudge teams toward refocusing and staying on mission.

Use of Psychology and Cultural Sensitivity
US Americans often advocate for direct approaches to conflict resolution; although, there are regional variations in methodology. People from the northeastern United States tend to be more direct, and people from the southeastern United States lean toward indirect communication. Some cultures, especially in the majority world, use mediators to help resolve conflict. Knowing the culture aids in conflict mediation. Jim Plueddemann's book, *Leading Across Cultures* provides great guidance in how to work in different global contexts. It is imperative to know your audience and to be sensitive to cultural norms.

Use of Wisdom

My friend, Paul Petrie, works with governmental leaders, members of parliament, and European royals. Sir Paul told me he honed his negotiating skills in his home. When his kids were at odds with each other, he'd serve as a mediator. He would have one child repeat the other's position to their satisfaction; then he'd repeat the process with the other child. Once each could clearly present the other's point of view with their approval, he knew he could then guide them toward reconciliation. The skills he developed as a father served him well in working with international leaders.

Sir Paul also told me resolution cannot occur unless people are willing to die to their own agendas. Conflicts need to be sieved through the cross. Most people would rather compromise and come to an agreement than to lay down their position. Movement toward Jesus is needed for true oneness to result. The Apostle Paul and John Mark model for us moving toward the cross—the result—unity.

JOURNAL TIME

Give an example of team conflict you've experienced.

How was the conflict handled?

What would you do differently today?

Week 3 Day 5: The Reproductive System: How Teams Multiply

The ultimate goal of MATTs is to multiply disciples, leaders, churches and movements. There are two ways to multiply. One way is promiscuous and the other is through a loving covenant relationship. Churches who want growth without commitment settle for larger crowds for numbers sake. However, loving relationships produce healthy families and churches. MATTs desire to see expansion rooted in godly relationships. Balancing the tension between relational growth and missional expansion requires skilled, mature, leaders who love one another.

Parents bring children into the world, build them up in their home, and eventually send them out of the home and into the world. The season in the home includes years of formal and informal instruction. After a couple of decades, the kids leave the nest, become parents themselves, and the parenting baton is passed. MATTs reproduction system functions in the same way.

Completion of Training Cycle

All eight of the teams utilize curriculum or systems of training. MATTs measure their success by completing the cycle. Completion means the trainees not only learn the material themselves, but they demonstrate competency in training other nationals through the material. The cycle is considered incomplete if it is only learned by the students. Four generations of learning is expected.

My mom, Ruby Dorman, had eight children. I came along when she was 42 years old. I was an uncle before I was born. My oldest brother is 23 years ahead of me. We have a picture of my mom with four generations of her descendants—five generations total. MATTs hope to live long enough to see the fifth generation trained.

Pass the Baton
Like running a relay, the baton passes sequentially around the track. The first baton pass occurs when a team trains the first generation of trainees. In leg two of the race, the trainees become trainers as the runner passes the baton to a third runner. The fourth runner crosses the finish line. The baton passes from runner one to runners two, three, and four. At four generations multiplication has occurred and a movement is possible. Read 2 Timothy 2:2 again.

> **2 Timothy 2:2 NASB**
> "The things which you have heard from me in the presence of many witnesses, entrust these to faithful people who will be able to teach others also."

When four generations are reached, MATTs are ready to exit a field and move on to new territory. However, the moving on is not a break in the relationships. Like grandparents who long to see their grandkids, the connection remains between trainers and trainees. MATTs are not simply utilitarian; they are relational. As the human body needs a healthy respiratory, circulatory, nervous, and reproductive system, MATTs need the same. For a team to form, function, deal with conflict, and reproduce, all four systems must be operative. In the book of Acts, we see all four systems working together.

The 5 P—Pattern of the Book of Acts
Acts begins and ends with declaration of the kingdom of God (Acts 1:3; Acts 28:31). Throughout the book the author, Luke, outlines how the kingdom grows. The first seven chapters outline Peter's influence. Chapter eight through chapter twenty-eight, Luke emphasizes Paul's ministry. Paul proves to be the most influential cross-cultural worker in the Bible. God includes Paul in taking the message beyond being a Jewish sect to a global audience including the Gentile world.

In Acts 1-7, Peter rises as the primary spokesman for the kingdom, he implements the pattern he observed in Jesus' ministry.

The pattern includes **proclamation** of the gospel of the kingdom, **prayer, power encounters, persecution** or opposition to the message or messengers, and **population increase**; the 5 P Pattern repeats nearly 20 times in the book of Acts. Below, we show two examples of the pattern: one during Peter's ministry and one during Paul's.

For an example during Peter's ministry **Read Acts 4:1-31.**
- **Proclamation** Acts 4:2—Bring them in—the Gospel message is *spoken*
- **Prayer** Acts 4:29—31—Build them up—God's people *pray*
- **Power** Acts 4:30—31– Send them out—God shows up and *changes* lives
- **Persecution** Acts 4:3—Publicly—There is *opposition*
- **Population** Increase 4:4—House to House—The Kingdom *multiplies*

Paul embraces the same pattern he sees in Peter's ministry. Acts 16 reveals the 5 step pattern clearly.

Read Acts 16:11-24
- **Proclamation** Acts 16:14—15—Bring them in—the Gospel message is *spoken*
- **Prayer** Acts 16:13 —Build them up—God's people *pray*
- **Power** Acts 16:18 Send them out—God shows up and *changes* lives
- **Persecution** Acts 16:17—Publicly—There is *opposition*
- **Population Increase** Acts 16:15—House to House—The Kingdom *multiplies*

Homes served as the locus of ministry in the early church. The far right column below provides references indicating when homes were used in ministry. Notice the use of homes in the early church was ubiquitous.

Acts	Bring them in (Father) Proclamation Evangelism	Build them up (Son) Prayer & Teaching Discipleship	Send them out (Holy Spirit) Power Encounter Ministry	Publicly Persecution (Suffering) Leadership and Worship	House to House Population Increase—Persuasion Fellowship
Chapter 1	8, 22	1, 14	3, 6, 16	13, 20, 25	13, 25
Chapter 2	11, 21, 23-24, 31-32, 38, 41	42-47	1-4, 17-20, 22, 43	14, 37	46
Chapter 3	12, 15, 19	1	6-10	22, 25	25
Chapter 4	2, 9-12, 31, 33	13, 23-31	7-8, 16, 30, 33	2, 18, 21, 36-37	4
Chapter 5	30-32	21, 25	5-11, 12, 15-16, 19, 33, 40-41	4, 17-18, 26-29	14, 42
Chapter 6	2	4, 6	8	5, 9-15	1, 7
Chapter 7	1-53	33	3, 36	9-10, 54-60	17
Chapter 8	4-5, 12, 22, 25, 35, 40	15, 24	6-8, 15, 26, 29, 39	1-3	3, 12, 38

Chapter 9	17,19-20-22, 27-28	10-11, 25, 31, 36, 40,	3, 10, 12, 15-16, 17-19, 29, 30, 34	1-9, 15-16, 23-24	18, 31, 35, 42
Chapter 10	28-33, 34-43	2-4, 9, 30	9-23, 38, 44-48	1, 9	6, 23, 32, 48
Chapter 11	14, 19-21	5, 26	7, 12, 15-16, 19, 27-30	2, 4, 22, 25	11, 12, 18, 24
Chapter 12	24	5, 12	7-11, 17	1-5,	12, 24
Chapter 13	5, 16, 22, 26, 29-35, 38, 47	1-3	1-3, 4, 8, 11, 52	9, 13, 36, 50	12, 43, 48
Chapter 14	1, 7, 15-18, 21, 25	22-23, 27-28	3, 8-10, 20	2, 4-5, 18, 19	1
Chapter 15	7, 11, 14, 17	35	3, 8, 12, 22, 25, 28, 33	1-6, 13, 19, 36, 37-41	14, 17
Chapter 16	10, 14, 31	13, 16, 25-29, 40	6-10, 16-24, 30	1-5, 19-24, 35-40	5, 14-15, 32-34
Chapter 17	2-3, 11, 13, 17-18, 23-31	11	10, 14, 32	5, 6-9, 13	4, 5, 12, 34
Chapter 18	4-5, 19, 27-28	23	9-11	6, 12, 17	7-8
Chapter 19	6, 10	7-10	6, 11-12	21-41	20
Chapter 20	21, 24	1-3, 20, 32, 36	7-16, 22-23, 25	4-6, 16, 20, 28-38	20
Chapter 21	19	4, 5, 8-14	4	18, 27-40	5-6, 8, 15, 20, 25
Chapter 22	16, 21	17	6-11, 21	1-30	16
Chapter 23	6		11	1-11, 12-35	
Chapter 24	14-15, 21, 24-27			1-27	

Chapter 25	19		25, 27	1-27	
Chapter 26	8-11, 17-18, 20, 28-29		12-18	1-26	28
Chapter 27	25	29, 35	23-24	1-44	
Chapter 28	23, 28, 31	8, 31	5, 8, 25	1-31	24

5 P CHART OF ACTS

Following the 5 P pattern found in the book of Acts lays a great foundation for multiplying leaders, teams, churches, and movements around the world. The Key Word is MULTIPLY—our job is to develop followers of Jesus Christ until he returns. In the book of Revelation, John speaks of a multitude. To have a multitude, we must multiply.

Revelation 5:9-10 (ESV)
"And they sang a new song, saying, 'Worthy are you to take the scroll and to open its seals, for you were slain, and by your blood you ransomed people for God from every tribe and language and people and nation, and you have made them a kingdom and priests to our God, and they shall reign on the earth.'"

God's desire includes "every tribe, language, people, and nation" becoming "a kingdom of priests." Our final week of study begins with the end in mind—all nations. Our kids used to play a game called, "Where in the world is Carmen Sandiego?" Brøderbund Software created the game to educate children about geography. We created **Kingdom Discipleship** to educate the church of God's heart for the world.

JOURNAL TIME

Take a moment. Pull out your journal. Where in the world does God want you? Ask him to give you a burden for somewhere in the world in addition to your current zip code. Write down what area of the world comes to mind. Don't make it too spiritual.

Where would you like to go?

What do you like about the area?

Do you like the food? What's your favorite dish?

Have you always been curious about place X. Maybe the geography or climate appeals to you. I typically look for places with good surf. I also am drawn to Europe.

Once you determine a location you feel drawn to, do some research. Google the area, the people, the language, the customs. Watch some travel shows about the location.

Two excellent resources are the Joshua Project and Operation World.

Check out the Joshua Project—https://joshuaproject.net/

Go to Operation World—https://www.operationworld.org/

Both The Joshua Project and Operation World provide details about peoples of the world. Pray for the area you are researching. Write out your prayers in your journal.

Once you have taken these steps, watch to see what happens next.

To impact the world with the good news of the kingdom, offer yourself to God's global plan. Then, take your next step. If you would like to have our team train with your small group or church, please contact us:

dougd@gtn.org

About the Author

We live between the inauguration of the kingdom, "the already", and the consummation of the kingdom, "not yet". Kingdom Discipleship seeks to make more and better disciples until Jesus return. Douglas and Joan Dorman formed Your Next Step as a discipleship ministry in 2004 after 17 years as church planters. Turning Disciples into Disciple Makers describes the lives of Douglas and Joan Dorman. Together, they teach, train, mentor, and coach others in discipleship, prayer, and leader development. The Dormans utilize a relational—life on life—approach to discipleship and emphasize the importance of using one's home as base for ministry. They have seven children and a growing number of grandchildren.

Douglas completed his PhD in Intercultural Studies at Biola University and Joan graduated with a BSN is nursing from the University of North Carolina Chapel Hill. Douglas and Joan currently serve as Senior Staff with Global Training Network http://www.gtn.org. To schedule discipleship training with your group email dougd@gtn.org

www.ingramcontent.com/pod-product-compliance
Lightning Source LLC
LaVergne TN
LVHW051814080426
835513LV00017B/1954